NOW THANK WE ALL OUR GOD

Organ Music for Praise and Thanksgiving

Edited by
C. H. TREVOR

This volume was first published under the title
Organ Music for Services of Thanksgiving

Music Department
OXFORD UNIVERSITY PRESS
Oxford and New York

CONTENTS

page

Ein' feste Burg ist unser Gott
(A Mighty Fortress is our God)

Chorale prelude	Reger	3
Chorale prelude	Kauffmann	4
Chorale prelude	J. C. Bach	6
Chorale prelude	Merkel	7
Chorale prelude	Buxtehude	8
*Chorale prelude	Walther	11
Chorale prelude	Pachelbel	12

Gelobt sei Gott
(God be praised)

Chorale prelude	Willan	14

Herr Gott, dich loben alle wir
(Lord God, we all give praise to Thee)

Chorale prelude	Walther	16
Chorale prelude	Pachelbel	18

Lobe den Herren, den mächtigen König der Ehren
(Praise to the Lord, the Almighty, the King of creation)

Chorale prelude	Reger	20
Chorale prelude	Merkel	21
Chorale prelude	Walther	22
Toccata	Micheelsen	24

Nun danket alle Gott
(Now thank we all our God)

*Chorale prelude	Oley	26
Chorale from Cantata No. 79	J. S. Bach	27
*Chorale prelude	Kauffmann	30
Chorale prelude	Reger	32

*Manuals only

Chorale prelude, "Ein' feste Burg ist unser Gott."
("A Mighty Fortress is our God.")

Max Reger

Chorale prelude, "Ein' feste Burg ist unser Gott."
("A Mighty Fortress is our God.")

Man. Diapasons 8. 4. 2. Mixture(s).
Ped. 16. 8. 4. Reed(s) 16. (8.) [or Reed(s) 16. (8.) alone.]
Man. + Ped.

G. F. Kauffmann (1679—1735)

Allegro moderato

Alternative registration:
R.H. Gt. Diapasons 8. 4. (2.)
L.H. Sw. Diapasons 8. 4. 2. (Mixture.)
Ped. 16. 8. 4. Reed 16. [or Reed(s) 16. (8.) alone.]
Gt. & Sw. to Ped.

The manuals should be equally balanced but different in tone quality.

Chorale prelude, "Ein' feste Burg ist unser Gott."
("A Mighty Fortress is our God.")

Gt. Diapasons 8. 4. 2.
Ped. 16. 8.
Gt. to Ped.

J. C. Bach (1642–1703)
uncle of J. S. Bach

Chorale prelude, "Ein' feste Burg ist unser Gott."
("A Mighty Fortress is our God.")

Gustav Merkel (1827–1885)

Chorale prelude, "Ein' feste Burg ist unser Gott."
("A Mighty Fortress is our God.")

I *f*
II *mf*
Ped. 16. 8. + II

Buxtehude (1637–1707)

Alternative registration:
I Gt. Trumpet 8. Mixture.
II Sw. Diapasons 8. 4. 2. (Mixture.)
Ped. 16. 8. + II

Chorale prelude, "Ein' feste Burg ist unser Gott."
("A Mighty Fortress is our God.")

Diapasons 8. 4. 2. (Mixture.)

J. G. Walther (1684–1748)

Chorale prelude, "Ein' feste Burg ist unser Gott."
("A Mighty Fortress is our God.")

Gt. Diapasons 8. 4. 2.
Ped. 16. 8.
Gt. to Ped.

J. Pachelbel (1653–1706)

Chorale prelude, "Gelobt sei Gott."
("God be praised.")

Healey Willan

© Copyright 1950 by Concordia Publishing House, St. Louis, Missouri. Reprinted by permission.

Chorale prelude, "Herr Gott, dich loben alle wir."
("Lord God, we all give praise to Thee.")

J. G. Walther (1684–1748)

Man. Diapasons 8. 4. 2. Mixture(s).
Ped. 16. 8. 4. Reed(s) 16. (8.) [or Reed(s) 16. (8.) alone.]
Man. + Ped.

Allegro moderato

Alternative registration:
Gt. Diapasons 8. 4. 2.
Sw. Diapasons 8. 4. 2. Reed(s). [or Reed(s) alone.]
Ped. 16. 8.
Gt. & Sw. to Ped.

Chorale prelude, "Herr Gott, dich loben alle wir."
("Lord God, we all give praise to Thee.")

Gt. (or Ch.) Flute 4. both hands.
Ped. coupled to Sw. Principal 4.
[Gt. (or Ch.) to Ped.]

This piece can effectively be played either loudly or softly.

J. Pachelbel (1653—1706)

Alternative registrations:
Gt. Diapasons 8. 4. 2.
Sw. Diapasons 8. 4. 2. Reed 8. [or Reed(s) alone.]
Ped. 16. 8.
Gt. & Sw. to Ped.

Gt. & Sw. Diapasons 8. 4. 2. Mixtures.
Ped. 16. 8. 4. Reeds 16. 8. [or Reed(s) 16. (8.) alone.]
Sw. to Gt.
Gt. & Sw. to Ped.

Chorale prelude, "Lobe den Herren, den mächtigen König der Ehren."
("Praise to the Lord, the Almighty, the King of creation.")

Max Reger

If preferred, this piece can be played *f* or *ff* throughout without change of registration.

Chorale prelude, "Lobe den Herren, den mächtigen König der Ehren."
("Praise to the Lord, the Almighty, the King of creation.")

Gustav Merkel (1827–1885)

Chorale prelude, "Lobe den Herren, den mächtigen König der Ehren."
("Praise to the Lord, the Almighty, the King of creation.")

Gt. Diapasons 8. 4. (2.)
Sw. Diapasons 8. 4. 2. (Mixture.)
Ped. 16. 8.
Sw. to Gt.
Gt. & Sw. to Ped.

J. G. Walther (1684–1748)

Allegro moderato (♩ = 72)

Alternative registrations:
Gt. & Sw. Diapasons 8. 4. 2. Mixtures.
Ped. {(32.) 16. 8. 4. Reed(s) 16. (8.)
or Reeds (32.) 16. 8. alone.}
Sw. to Gt.
Gt. & Sw. to Ped.

Gt. Diapasons 8. 4. 2. (Mixture.)
Sw. Reed(s) (16.) 8. (4.)
Ped. 16. 8.
Gt. & Sw. to Ped.

Toccata, "Lobe den Herren, den mächtigen König der Ehren."
("Praise to the Lord, the Almighty, the King of creation.")

Hans Friedrich Micheelsen

Reprinted by permission of Bärenreiter – Verlag, Kassel.

Chorale prelude, "Nun danket alle Gott."
("Now thank we all our God.")

Gt. Diapasons 8. 4. (2.)

J. C. Oley (died 1789)

Alternative registration:
Gt. Diapasons 8. 4. 2. coupled to Sw. Diapasons 8. 4. 2. (Mixture.)

Chorale from Cantata No. 79, "Nun danket alle Gott."
("Now thank we all our God.")

I Gt. *f*
II Sw. *mf*
Ped. 16. 8.
Sw. to Ped.

J. S. Bach (1685–1750)

Maestoso

Alternative registrations:
I Gt. Trumpet 8.
II Sw. Diapasons 8. 4. 2. (Mixture.)
Ped. 16. 8.
Sw. to Gt.
Sw. to Ped.

I Solo. Tuba(s) 8. (4.)
II Diapasons 8. 4. 2. Mixture(s).
Ped. 16. 8. 4. + II

Chorale prelude, "Nun danket alle Gott."
("Now thank we all our God.")

Diapasons 8. 4. 2.

G. F. Kauffmann (1679–1735)

Chorale prelude, "Nun danket alle Gott."
("Now thank we all our God.")

Max Reger

If preferred, this piece can be played *f* or *ff* throughout without change of registration.